FLORIDA GIRLS

Nancy Hasty

I0139941

BROADWAY PLAY PUBLISHING INC
New York
www.broadwayplaypublishing.com
info@broadwayplaypublishing.com

Cover photo by Carol Rosegg
First printing: June 2014
I S B N: 978-0-88145-584-7
Book design: Marie Donovan
Page make-up: Adobe Indesign
Typeface: Palatino
Printed and bound in the U S A

FLORIDA GIRLS opened on 21 June 1990 at the
Theater Arielle in New York City, presented by Eric
Krebs. The cast and creative contributors were:

Performer ....Nancy Hasty

Director.. Bob Stewart

Set & production management .... E F Morrill

Sound .... J Bloomrosen

Stage manager.. Lloyd Davis Jr

CHARACTERS & SETTING

all the characters are played by one performer

AUNT LOIS, *45,* DALE's *sister, rough and gruff with a dead-eyed stare*

SUSIE VAN HELMS, *12, the middle child, misunderstood, a martyr*

DOREEN VAN HELMS, *40, the mother of 5 girls, alive, energized, always in motion*

CHRISTINE VAN HELMS, *17, the eldest daughter, haughty and aloof*

DEE DEE VAN HELMS, *16, at times hysterical, sometimes unintelligible*

DIXIE VAN HELMS, *8,* SUSIE's *shadow, and a master spy*

EULENE HENDERSON, *70s, the sorrowful, fearful neighbor next door*

LEE-ANN VAN HELMS, *only 3, but with a will of iron*

DALE VAN HELMS, *48, the father of 5 girls, good looking, a gunslinger*

DUANE HEINEY, *14, an outlaw, a young James Dean*

WAYNE HEINEY, *his twin brother*

GRANDMOTHER, DOREEN's *mother, 70s, fiery with faith*

REVEREND THOMPSON, *60s, but going strong*

BOBBI BOLAND, *a tad over 30, but still a contender*

THE M C, *50s, also the high school principal*

The play takes place in the mid-60s in a small town in the Florida panhandle.

The author gratefully acknowledges the following people who assisted in the development of FLORIDA GIRLS: James H Mayer, Kevin Andrews, Susan Gregg, Elizabeth Perry—and especially her family.

For my husband, Ray,
with love and gratitude.

ACT ONE

Scene One

(Spotlight rises AUNT LOIS *sitting in a chair. She is gruff, rough, down-to-earth and in control. She has a thick Southern accent and a dead-eyed stare.)*

AUNT LOIS: Susie, your daddy has come to me and told me you your mind is made up to go to New York City to become an *actress!* And he's asked me to talk to you on account of the fact I've been to New York. *(Pause)* I know it was one time.

I know it was for one day.

But you ain't got to be in a place for years to know what it's like unless you're a fool. Now, let me tell you something about your New York City! *(As the great oracle)* Vince and I was there that time we had that layover at La-guard-eee-yah. And Vince had to do some shopping! Now, what was the name of where we went. There's a name for it. This is gonna bother me... Jesse, open that garage door. *(Yelling)* Vince! *(Shaking her head)* He ain't gonna remember...

Anyway and anyhow, it was a part of Manhattan that had...*shops.* All these little staircases going up and down. So we went up and down the stairs and there was a sign on the door that said, "ring the buzzer". So we rang the buzzer, and directly a woman she come and unlocked the door and let us in. *(Sitting bolt upright)* Did you get that? This was in broad daylight.

She had to *unlock* the door to let us in. Susie, in New York City the bad people roam the streets and the good people are locked up!!

Now, I know what your daddy is concerned about. He is terrified you're gonna go up to New York City and turn hard. I'm not saying a thing in the world against Yankee women! I'm sure every last one of them is a fine, Christian woman. But you've got to admit, they are abrupt! *(Sharing a great secret)* I've got a personal theory on that. I think it's because of the weather. Well, their winters are so snowy, and sleety and rainy and cold and nasty and all—and you should bear that in mind—they can't stand out on the streets and be pleasant the way we can. No, they just have to go: *(In clipped, harsh accent:)* Hi! Hi! How are you? Fine! Fine! See you later. Bye! Bye! *(Sitting back)* And by the time spring rolls around, they just stay snappy all year long! Now, I know you want to be an *actress*! And I think you're good. The way you do that poem, "The Highway," just sets my teeth on edge. I get chills up and down my arms.

But have you thought what you could have if you stayed right here in Claryville, Florida? Well, just hear me out. Just a minute— *(Talking over* SUSIE*)* You could teach dramatics at the high school, and those kids would love you! Just listen! You would have— *(Counting off on her fingers)* —major med, a dental plan, three months off in the summer to do whatever you wanted to do. Hold on! If you still wanted to perform, you could rejoin the Claryville Curtain Pullers, they've done some outstanding productions— *(Wounded)* Well! The last thing I wanted to be was a nosy parker. The last thing I wanted to do was crush a dream. But your daddy asked me to talk to you because he and Doreen love you. *(Pause)* And Vince and I love you. And Jesse and Johnny. *(Pause)* Corrie and Paul. Linda and Earl. Pete and Esther. *(As an afterthought)* Beulah, Ben, Larry,

Mae, Skip, Sally— *(There's more)* Debbie, Mel, Duke, Donnie... *(Misty-eyed)* We all just love you. And we want you to be happy.

SUSIE: *(Standing)* I love you, too, Aunt Lois. But I'm going. *(To the audience)* And boy, I went. But I do go back. I go back often. Sometimes I visit the old house we lived in when I was twelve. I can still see the screen door to the kitchen and hear my mother's voice...

(The lights shift and DOREEN *can be seen entering the kitchen.)*

(End of Scene One)

Scene Two

(Lights rise full. DOREEN, *is alive, robust, energized.)*

DOREEN: *(Singing)* "On top of old Smokey, all covered with snow..." *(Clapping her hands)* Hey! Who wants to go to the Great Smokey Mountains? *(Calling up the stairs)* Christine, Dee Dee, Susie, Dixie, Lee-Ann! Let's go! *(At the door)* Dale, you 'bout got those black-eyed peas picked? Well, just fill that one box. I'm gonna get the girls to shell 'em on the way. *(Stepping out onto the porch)* Oh, and baby, leave out some we drop off at Mama's house. *(Lowering her voice:)* No, I haven't told the girls we're stopping by her house. *(Re-entering)* It's not going to kill them to visit with their grandmother... it didn't kill you! *(Kicking the door back open)* Dale! I heard that! *(In the house, looking out the window)* Now what is he saying to me? What? What, baby? No, you go on and get the car tanked up. We'll be sitting on ready when you get back. *(To herself)* We'll be sitting on ready if I can get me some help down here. *(Clapping her hands again)* Girls! Girls! Christine, Dee Dee, Susie, Dixie, Lee-Ann! Let's go! *(Angrily)* Christine? CHRISTINE!

(CHRISTINE *appears. She is 17, haughty and aloof.*)

CHRISTINE: I'm here, *Mother.* You needn't screech.
Mother, someone's been into my things again. And
I just don't appreciate it when other people — who
don't appreciate their things get into mine. I just don't
appreciate it. *(Sitting)* Mother, I thought I told you, Dee
Dee and I are staying here. Oh, yes we are! And these
are the reasons why. *(Itemizing on her fingers)* One, I am
seventeen and Dee Dee is sixteen and I guess we're old
enough to look out for ourselves.

Two, Eulene is just next door, if you want to get
particular about it. Three, and most importantly, the
Miss Claryville Beauty Pageant is in seven days and
there's too much that has to be done. I'll tell you what
has to be done! *(Itemizing on her other hand)* A—Bobbi
Boland has to fit us again for our dresses. B—she's
promised to work with us on our walks and our
pivots. C—we need to practice our talents. *(Exploding)*
MOTHER! Since when will the piano FIT in a station
wagon?

DOREEN: Christine, just climb down off your high horse
and go in the pantry and get the breakfast things in
the ice chest. *(Muttering)* As if we'd leave two young
girls alone in a house while we are hundreds of miles
away—Christine, did you hear anybody say we were
going by Grandmother's? *(She has crossed to the counter
and is busy making sandwiches.)* Well, I'm just asking
you! *(Changing the subject)* Now, where is Dee Dee? Dee
Dee?

(DEE DEE, *16, appears. She is so hysterical, she is
unintelligible. She screams, weeps and gestures wildly.*)

DEE DEE: *MOTHER!!!!!!!!!!!!!!!!!!!!!!!!!!!* *(The rest is
garbled)*

DOREEN: Dee Dee, you're going to have to catch hold of
yourself. I can't understand a word you are saying.

DEE DEE: My eye! Look at my eye! *(More hysteria)*

DOREEN: Well, look up. Well it is. It's the beginning of a sty. Sug, I don't know if it's going to clear up before the pageant. Don't touch it! It's not going to clear up if you play with it. Now, until you can calm down, go on over there and finish making up those sandwiches for the road. *(To* CHRISTINE*)* I declare she is going to *have* to catch hold of herself! *(Glancing at* DEE DEE*)* Whoa! Whoa! how many pieces of lunchmeat did you put on there? Dee Dee Van Helms, you've got on *three* pieces of Oliveloaf! Is that how you do when I'm not here? No wonder, I'm always running out! *(Talking over* DEE DEE*)* Fine, fine, fine. When you've got your own house and *you're* footing the bills you can put on ten for all I care. But right now, one is sufficient! *(Glancing out the door)* Lord help me, Dixie is outside naked as a jaybird! Dixie, get up those stairs and get some clothes on this minute. *(Looking outside again)* And the clothes are still on the clothesline. What did you girls do last night— not a single thing got done! *(At the stairs)* Susie? Susie? *(To* DIXIE*)* Yes, Dixie, get those on! Susie, come down, I need you to bring in the clothes.

*(*SUSIE *comes down the stairs. She is 12 years old, the middle child, and misunderstood. She is also sulky, morose and a martyr.)*

SUSIE: GAH, Mother. Why do I always have to be the one to bring in the clothes? Gah. Why can't I do what Christine's doing? *(Listening to her mother)* Gah. Why can't I do what Dee Dee's doing? *(Listening)* Gah. Why don't I ever get a good job? *(Whirling on* DEE DEE*)* What, Dee Dee? *(Pointing and jeering)* Pink eye! Dee Dee's got the pink eye!

DOREEN: Susie, cut that out. Now come out here and —Dixie! *(Grabbing* DIXIE*)* Don't you run through this house!

(DIXIE, 8 years old and a hellion has buck teeth and a glint in her eye.)

DIXIE: Sorry!

DOREEN: Come here and help Susie bring in the clothes.

SUSIE: Not Dixie! Gah, Mother, why do I always get Dixie? *GOD* — just forget it.

DOREEN: What did you say? *(Snapping SUSIE to her)* That is NOT what you said. And I've got news for you—I don't even like "gah!" Now, march outside and bring in the clothes— *(Calling after them)* and make sure you leave your daddy's slacks on the slack-stretcher! *(Watching Dixie climb)* Dixie, get down from that tetherball pole! Get down! *(Smiling)* I declare, I know she wishes she'd been born a boy. *(Seeing EULENE)* Oh, no! It's Eulene coming through the hedge.

CHRISTINE: Mother, she's a depressant!!

DEE DEE: Mother, I wouldn't believe anything that woman said to me!!

DOREEN: Both of you just get back to work and let me handle this. *(At the door)* Hey, Eulene, well, we're kind of in a hurry. We're trying to get off on our trip to the Great Smokey Mountains to see Dale's sister Edna—

(But EULENE has managed to enter. In her 70s, she is a sorrowful woman. She speaks in a nasal, hissing voice and keeps her arms wrapped fearfully around her thin body with one hand clutched at her throat.)

EULENE: Doreen, I wanted to come over last night, but Roberta said, nooooooo— *(Sounds like "new")* Eulene, it's too late. What? Your girls didn't tell you last night? Christine? Dee Dee? Doreen, do you know what we saw big as life in your front yard last night? A man! A big man! *(Excited)* Doreen, he was peeking in your picture window and then he just disappeared around the corner of your house. We called Sheriff Bob Tomlin

but you know how he is! He said, "Did you see Big
Foot again?" I said, "Sheriff Bob, this time it wasn't
the Heiney boys!" So he sent a cruiser out and that's
when the deputy talked to your two girls but they said
they didn't hear or see a thing! *(Moving to her)* Doreen,
did you hear about that poor woman in Pensacola last
week? *(Whispering)* Well, a man got into her house and
got her sewing scissors and hid under her bed. Later
on, when that poor woman was getting ready for bed,
getting into her *nightgown!* —he popped out and he
took her out back and he— *(She is whispering again, too
low to hear until she says, in tears)* …with her scissors!
(With vigor) So I just came over here to tell you that
we're gonna take care of your house while you're gone.
We're going to work relays by that window yonder
if we have to. Don't thank me, Doreen, that's what
neighbors are for! Ya'll just be careful driving…Roberta
heard on the radio this morning that a whole family
was *killed* out here on Highway 85. Well, Christine,
evidently their car stalled and then a semi came
up behind them and just ran all nine of them over!
(Starting out) Well, I'd better go. So ya'll just go on your
vacation—and have *fun!*

DOREEN: Good-bye! Thank you, Eulene!

CHRISTINE: Mother, she's a depressant!

DOREEN: Both of you girls get over here. What went on
here last night? We left you two big girls in charge and
—no, I don't want to hear about the Heiney Boys…
(Glancing behind) Lee-Ann, put down my pocketbook!

(LEE-ANN, *the baby, is sneaking off with* DOREEN's *purse.*
DOREEN *turns back to* CHRISTINE *and* DEE DEE.)

DOREEN: I don't care if she is hysterical— *(Glancing
behind again)* Lee-Ann, put down my pocketbook! *(To
the girls)* Well, I think we have the right to know when
the police have been here! *(To* LEE-ANN) *Lee-Ann! Give*

me my billfold! (Snatching it) You never touch Mother's
billfold! *(Listening)* What do you need money for? Well,
Lee-Ann, Mama wants to talk to you about that place
on your behind.

(As the girls titter)

DOREEN: Girls! *(To* LEE-ANN*)* The doctor said to sit on
something on a long car ride—because it hurts, that's
right, baby, Mama knows. Lee-Ann, he said go to the
drug store and buy a little cushion because he doesn't
know we've got a whole garage full of inner-tubes.
Now go out there and get you one ready for the car.
Lee-Ann, we are not going to the drugstore! *(Opening
the door)* Now move! *(When she doesn't)* I am looking for
a switch. I am looking for good one!

(As LEE-ANN *takes off)*

DOREEN: That is the stubbornist four year old I've ever
laid eyes on! *(Re-entering:)* I wish you girls wouldn't
laugh at her. She's spoiled rotten enough as it is.
(Listening) Uh-oh! That's him. Yep, that's Daddy. Okay,
quick, Dee Dee, finish wrapping those sandwiches and
give Christine a hand with the ice chest, it's heavy!
Susie! Dixie! Bring in those clothes! Hurry! Daddy's
here! Just set them on my bed and don't wrinkle them.
Lee-Ann, get you an innertube!

(As CHRISTINE *and* DEE DEE *cross before* DOREEN*)*

DOREEN: Come on, Christine, pick up. I'll hold the door
for you. Christine, you are not staying here and that's
final!! Susie, just hit that light on your way out. Dixie!
You had all morning to go to the bathroom. Well, pull
'em up! Pull 'em up! *(Stepping outside)* Okay, Dale,
we're ready! *(Pointing)* Christine, Dee Dee, get that box
and—

CHRISTINE: *(Shocked)* Either those peas stay — or I do!

DEE DEE: Shell peas?????

SUSIE: Gah, Mother, just forget it!

DOREEN: I don't believe it. I just don't believe it. Is it going to kill you girls to shell a few peas while you're just sitting in a car? *(Talking over* DEE DEE*)* No, Dee Dee, No! I highly doubt that anyone is going to ride past us on the interstate and look down into our window and notice that you girls are shelling a few miserable black-eyed peas. And so what if they do? Do you know what I say? Big deal is what I say. Dale, can you talk? Can you say something?

*(*DALE, *a good looking man in his late 40s, is also a man of few words. He crosses like a gunslinger and speaks in a low, threatening voice.)*

DALE: Christine...Dee Dee... *(Staring them down)* PICK. UP. THAT. BOX. OF. PEAS. AND. GET. IT. IN. THE. CAR.

*(*DALE *watches them vanish with the box.)*

DALE: SUSIE! Back-back seat.

DIXIE. Likewise.

Lee-Ann? You want to get out of that innertube and get in the car?

(They have all disappeared. DALE *turns to* DOREEN *with a grin.)*

DALE: *(Singing:)* "Keep those doggies moving, Rawhide!"

*(*DOREEN *pretends not to be impressed as she crosses to the car.)*

DOREEN: Cowboy!

(End of Scene Two)

Scene Three

(A few moments later.

(Lights rise on DOREEN*arline as she gets into the station wagon and locks her door.)*

DOREEN: Okay, Lee-Ann, move your innertube just a little. *(Looking back)* Girls! Let's help Daddy back out. Move your heads. Move, your hair, Christine.

SUSIE: Yeah, Christine. Move your hair. *(Shoving* DIXIE*)* Dixie, get off my side of the seat!

DOREEN: Girls! Settle down. *(Reaching into the glove compartment)* Want a Sight-Saver, Dad? *(Handing him one)* I believe I'll have one, too.

*(*DOREEN *cleans her glasses, squinting as she polishes.)* Brrr. Dale, it's chilly in here. Turn off that air conditioner for a bit. *(Pause)* Well, I will! *(Turning it off)*

CHRISTINE: *(Screaming)* AIR!!!!!!!!!!!!!!

DEE DEE: AIR!!!!!!!!!!!!!!!!!!

SUSIE: GAH, MOTHER, CAN WE HAVE SOME AIR BACK HERE?????

DOREEN: *(Turning it back on)* Well, it's only staying on for a minute. It's like a refrigerator in here. My teeth are plumb chattering. *(Alarmed)* Dale! Do you see that stop sign? Well, stop!

(The car lurches to a stop. DOREEN *massages the back of her neck.)*

DOREEN: There's the Heiney Boys. Getting on their bikes.

DIXIE: Suspended! They had to suspend both of them 'cause they couldn't tell which one did it.

DOREEN: I'm not a bit surprised. Dale, they were bothering Eulene again last night. She had to call the police.

SUSIE: It wasn't the Heiney Boys!

CHRISTINE: *(To* SUSIE*)* Shut up!

*(*DOREEN *leans over and honks the horn.)*

DOREEN: Now, Dale, say something to them. Go on, say something to them!

DALE: *(Muttering)* Why do I have to say something to them? *(Getting out of the car)* Duane? Wayne! No, you're Wayne, sorry, Duane. Never can get you boys straight. How you boys doing?

(The HEINEY *boys are both 14 and outlaws. They both look like the young James Dean. Shirtless and fearless, they stand their ground with* DALE*.)*

DUANE: *(Spitting over his shoulder)* Fine. *(Peering into the car)* Hey, Mrs Van Helms. *(With disdain)* Christine. Dee Dee. *(Smiling, with meaning)* Hey, Susie. *(Back to* DALE*)* Sir? We ain't been no where near your yard last night, was we, Wayne? No sir! You ask Tommy Sapp, we were helping him change the oil in his car. You ask him, just ask him!

DALE: Well, Duane, all I'm saying is—you know—just—don't… *(He gets back into the car and glares at* DOREEN*.)* Why don't you mind your own business??

DOREEN: Well, Lee-Ann, we thought it was the Heiney Boys. Slow down, Dale, it's Miss Mildred. *(Rolling down her window)* Hey, Miss Mildred! Yard looks mighty pretty. We're going up to see Dale's sister, Edna. Bye! *(Thoughtfully)* Miss Mildred got Yard of the Month. Did you girls know Miss Mildred got Yard of the Month? Now, next weekend we're going to get some work done on our yard.

CHRISTINE: I'm not doing one stick of yardwork until after the pageant!

DEE DEE: *(In a rush)* And Daddy, you promised to build me a vanity table and I have to rehearse with it Thursday night and we won't be back until—

DOREEN: Dee Dee Dee Dee Dee Dee Dee Dee Dee Dee! Daddy said he would build you that vanity table Tuesday night. Dale, it doesn't have to be elaborate—

DEE DEE: LIGHTS!!! IT HAS TO HAVE LIGHTS!!!!

DALE: It always has to have something. And it's always Daddy that has to do it. Hand me a Stim-U-Dent, Mama.

(DALE waits until DOREEN hands him a toothpick. Then, with his eye on the rearview:)

DALE: Now after this contest is over, let that be it! This family's going to settle down. You don't see me and Mama going all the time.

DOREEN: It's not that we don't want you girls to take part and have. It's just that we all need to do our share—put our shoulder to the wheel and help carry the load. *(Glancing back)* You girls shelling? Well, Christine, hand me some up here. I enjoy shelling. *(Starting to shell)* Anybody want to sing? *(Smiling down at LEE-ANN)* What you want to sing, Lee-Ann? Sounds good to me. You want to start, Dad?

DALE: *(Singing)* "I love to go a wandering, along the mountain track…"

(DALE points to DOREEN with his toothpick.)

DOREEN: *(Singing)* "And as I go—"

(DOREEN pauses and nods her head in time as LEE-ANN sings. DOREEN now finishes the line:)

DOREEN: "My knapsack on my back."

(DOREEN points back to CHRISTINE to continue:)

CHRISTINE: *(Singing with an attitude)* "Val-a-ree… Val-a-rah…"

(CHRISTINE tosses her head towards DEE DEE.)

DEE DEE: *(Impossibly high)* "Val-a-reeeeeeeeeee"—

SUSIE: *(Singing)* "Val-a-rah-ha-ha-ha-ha-ha-ha-ha-ha—"

DIXIE: *(Singing)* "Val-a-ree… Val-a-rah… "

(DIXIE points back up to DALE, who gives a big finish:)

DALE: "My knapsack on my BACK!" Yeeeoooww! *(Basking in the glory)* Good enough for Arthur Godfrey!

(CHRISTINE suddenly leans up towards the front seat.)

CHRISTINE: Wait a minute. Wait one red-hot minute! Mother, I deliberately asked you this morning if we were going to Grandmother's and you said no. *(Turning to her sisters)* Ya'll, they're taking us to Grandmother's!

DEE DEE: Grandmother's???????????

SUSIE: Gah, Mother, just forget it!!

DOREEN: I don't believe it. I *don't* believe it. Is it going to kill you girls to stop by and visit with your grandmother for a few minutes? *(Angry)* Christine! Sit back and shell! I better not hear that again! *(Turning on DALE)* Dale, it's all your fault. They get it from you. Dale, she can't help the way she is! Dale, just hush. It's all fine and good to go visit your relatives but when I want to just stop by and see my mother for a few minutes—Dale, just hush! Well, you ought to be. *(Suddenly, eyes front)* DALE! YOU HIT HER FLAMINGO! *(She gets out of the car and investigates the plastic flamingo.)* Well, back up! *(Crossing to the front door)* I can't do it all, Lord. I just can't do it all. *(Knocking)* Mama? Mama, it's Doreen. I brought the girls to come see you. Mama? *(Crossing back to the car)* Roll it down. She must be down at the spring, so just

hold on. *(Straightening the flamingo again)* Mangled!
(Crossing the yard) Mama? It's Doreen! I've brought the
girls to come see you. Mama?

(Down in the thicket we can hear GRANDMOTHER as she
"figs." This is accomplished by using a long pole and
jamming it up into the fig trees.(

GRANDMOTHER: *(Singing)* "Marching as to war, with
the cross of Jesus—" *(Figging)* Come on down figs.
Come on down, Mister Figs! *(Listening)* Doreen! I do
know! You have finally come to see me.

(GRANDMOTHER *emerges from the woods and throws down
her figging pole. In her late 70's, she is almost frighteningly
alive and overpowering. Today she would be labeled bi-polar.
To her family now, she just seems manic and difficult. She
is also a religious fanatic.)* Get back, ducks. Get back, Mr.
Drake! *(Embracing her)* Doreen, I do know. I was talking
to the Lord this morning and I said, "Lord, bring
Doreen to see me!" And you are here! *(Gazing upward)*
Thank you, thank you, thank you! *(Crossing to the car)*

GRANDMOTHER: Hi there, Charles! *(Peering into the back
seat)* Hi there, Dee Dee. I do know, I have some pigs
feet I haven't even opened! *(Catching sight of* CHRISTINE*)*
Christine! Your hair! Doreen, it's too big. You need to
take a hairbrush to that! *(Opening the back of the station
wagon and yanking* DIXIE *and* SUSIE *out by their hands.)* Hi
there, Susie and Dixie! I do know, I am so glad to see
you.

DOREEN: *(Nervously)* Well, Mama, it's good to see you,
too. But we can only stay for a minute.

GRANDMOTHER: *(Shocked)* A minute? A min-ete?? *(To
Susie and* DIXIE*)* I thought you said you came to see me?

DOREEN: Well, Mama, we did. We're here. But we
promised Dale's sister Edna we'd go up and see her,
too. *(Meaningfully)* She's been sick, you know…

GRANDMOTHER: *(Pounding her bosom)* I HAVE NOT BEEN WELL!

(GRANDMOTHER begins to weep as she turns to DIXIE and SUSIE.) The next time you see me it will be at my funeral! Come on, babies!

(GRANDMOTHER takes DIXIE and SUSIE into her house, singing.)

GRANDMOTHER: "What a friend I have in *Jesus...* "

(DOREEN follows GRANDMOTHER in and takes her by the shoulders.)

DOREEN: Mama, please don't make this hard on me. Please! We would love to—

(DALE honks the horn and DOREEN crosses back outside to the car)

DOREEN: Dale Van Helms, don't you ever sound a horn at me again. Dale, I told you last night she's not going to try to jump in and come with us! What?

(DOREEN sees DIXIE, GRANDMOTHER and SUSIE crossing to the car.)

DOREEN: Susie, Dixie, put down that suitcase. Mama, put down that sack. *(Wrestling the sack from GRANDMOTHER)* Mama, we would love to have you come with us but we just don't have the room. We've got the girls and the luggage and the ice chest and there's just not enough room. But we did bring you something! *(Trying to open the door)* Christine — *unlock the door!* Now hand me that box of peas. Thank you, your highness! *(Crossing to GRANDMOTHER)* See, Mama, we brought you some peas—

(GRANDMOTHER is lunges towards the back seat.)

GRANDMOTHER: I will sit small!

DOREEN: No, Mama! *(Grabbing her)* You just can't come with us and that's that!

GRANDMOTHER: *(Sadly)* Well, since I can't go "whither you goest" —and since you will not stay... *(Smothering* DIXIE *and* SUSIE *to her bosom)* ...then let Susie and Dixie be with me!

DOREEN: Mama!!! *(Leading* DIXIE *off)* Dixie, you wouldn't want to stay with Grandmother, would you?

DIXIE: *(Grinning)* If Susie will!

*(*DOREEN *leads* SUSIE *off a few feet.)*

DOREEN: Susie... Dixie just said she would stay with Grandmother, if you would. *(Pitifully)* You don't have to if you don't want to...but...would you? *(Embracing her)* Susie, Mother *loves* you! *(Moving quickly to the car)* Dee Dee, hand me out that blue suitcase — the one next to the red one. *(Embracing* DIXIE*)* Now, Dixie, you mind Susie and be good. *(Embracing* GRANDMOTHER*)* Mama, make sure they eat right and get to bed early. We're counting on you.

DALE: Susie! Come here!

*(*DALE *rolls down the window and after discreetly taking a bill from his wallet, he palms it to* SUSIE *via a handshake. He winks at her.)*

DALE: Now, be sweet.

DOREEN: And Susie, we'll be back early Sunday evening. Now, ya'll take care. We love you! Bye.

(The car pulls away with DOREEN *sadly looking backwards. Then, brightly:)*

DOREEN: Well, they'll have a good time! *(Pause)* With what money, Christine? *(Wheeling on* DALE*)* Dale, how much did you give her?

*(*SUSIE *is left standing, sobbing quietly, watching the car vanish.)*

SUSIE: Mother!! (*She waves.*) (*A moment later she opens her hand to find one dollar bill. With great disappointment.*) Gah!

(*End of Scene Three*)

Scene Four

(*Lights rise dimly on* SUSIE *centerstage. This is the adult* SUSIE, *looking back.*)

SUSIE: I know it probably isn't true but it seems that every time we visited Grandmother's house it was either twilight or raining. Her house sat at the top of a hill and even then you had to fight the underbrush to find the door. The front door was completely overgrown so we entered what she referred to as "the breezeway". The windows were small, jalousie windows that you rolled in and out and inside the breezeway—stacked from the floor to the ceiling—was every magazine and newspaper she'd ever owned. And the first sense you had as you entered was that of—mildew.

Then there was a long, dark hall. On one side of the hallway was a sideboard and stacked on that sideboard was everything from clothing and needles and thread and thimbles to photographs of grandchildren, postcards from National Parks—church fans with Jesus kneeling in the Garden of Gethsemane one side and "Jessup's Funeral Home" on the other.

On the right were two bedrooms. When I was in high school Grandmother sold one of my friends she had to board up the bedrooms. When my friend asked why, Grandmother said, "Oh, honey! The rats got so bad. On Saturday night I laid out my good hat on the bed to be ready for church on Sunday morning and in the night—Mr. Rat ate my hat!"

Mother—did you know there were *rats* in her house we
when had to stay with her?
On the right is also a bathroom. The tub is old
fashioned with claws for feet. Grandmother keeps
her clothes folded and stored in the bathroom until
its time for our baths. Then we take the clothes out
of the bathtub *(She mimes this.)* and get in the bathtub
and scrub each other's backs in the dark while
Grandmother sits on the commode and sings,

"Bringing in the Sheaves"—in the dark!

At the end of the long dark hall is the kitchen. For
as long as I can remember Grandmother had a
refrigerator but she still referred to it as "the box."
(Imitating GRANDMOTHER*)* Honey, look in the *box* on
the second shelf, in the far corner on the right side,
behind the collard greens, in a small blue bowl and see
if you see the… "

*(*SUSIE*'s voice trails off as* GRANDMOTHER *begins to stir a
pot on the stove.)*

GRANDMOTHER: *(Singing:)* "… an emblem of suffering
and shame, and I love that old cross, where the dearest
and best… " *(Calling)* Dixie! Honey, sugarbaby! I need
you to call Susie to bring in the figs.

*(*DIXIE *starts outside with her hand on the porch light
switch.)*

GRANDMOTHER: NO!! Don't turn on the light! Every
time you turn on a light, it costs a dime!

DIXIE: So??? *(She steps outside into the shadows.)* Susie?
Grandmother said to bring in the figs. *(No answer)*
SUSIE? Grandmother said to bring in the figs! *(Growing
frightened)* SUSIE??? *(Spying* SUSIE*)* Susie! Why didn't
you answer me?

SUSIE: *(In tears:)* Damn these mosquitoes. Damn these
briars! Damn these figs!

DIXIE: Foot, you ain't done nothing. How would you like to give Grandmother a bath?) Scrub-a-dub-dub! We had to come out here and get pots and pans of rainwater and then I had to help Grandmother wash her hair. Only she only washed half of it—to save on water!

(As GRANDMOTHER *appears on the porch)*

DIXIE: We're coming! *(Whispering to* SUSIE*)* And then, guess what? She put on Granddaddy's underwear!

(They enter. DIXIE *hands* GRANDMOTHER *the bucket of figs.)*

DIXIE: I got her!

GRANDMOTHER: Thank you! Now, Susie…sugarbaby…I need you to take this Brillo pad and go yonder to the sideboard and you see my hairpins? I need you to scrub the rust off the hairpins—with the Brillo pad! *(She hands* SUSIE *the Brillo pad.)* And Dixie, sugarbaby, you keep looking through that drawer until you find me one good stocking. And with his help *(Pointing heavenward)* I will put on the peas. Help me Lord! Help me. Lord help me!

*(*GRANDMOTHER *exits.* DIXIE *watches her leave with glee. She advances to the bureau still laughing. After opening the drawer, she takes out a stocking only to find it filled with runs.)*

DIXIE: Nope! *(Looking at another)* Nope! *(And another)* Nope! Pssst! Hey, Nance, why doesn't she just buy new stockings? Pssst, hey Nance? What doesn't she buy new bobbypins? Hee-hee! *(She imitates* SUSIE*'s scrubbing of the hairpins.)* Pssst, hey Nance—how much money did Daddy give you? Half that's mine, you know. Let's see, I could use some B Bs and some comic books and some—

SUSIE: *(Scrubbing furiousl)* For your information, that money is mine—all mine! Is too! You stupid little brat, don't you see, he was paying me to stay with you. Only he should have made it a hundred dollars!

DIXIE: Oh yeah? Well, maybe if he'd paid the girls last night they wouldn't have locked you out of the house. Ha-ha! Eulene thought you were a *man!*

(As SUSIE chases her)

DIXIE: Susie got locked out! Susie got locked out!

(As SUSIE grabs her hair and pulls)

DIXIE: Ouch! Help! Let me go! Grandmother!!!

GRANDMOTHER: Yes? I do know! *(Pulling them apart)* "Love thy neighbor as thyself!" Now, did you find me one more good stocking? *(Taking one from DIXIE)* Thank you! *(Sitting and putting it on)* I just put those peas on low so they can cook while we are gone. *(To SUSIE)* Why, honey we are going to the Church. I do know, it is Revival Week at the Church and we will be there nightly! Now, let me see the hairpins. *(Holding one up to the light)* Oh, Susie, what a good job you have done. They are clean as a whistle! Now, you just put them in my hair wherever you think it needs it. *(Pulling her hair into a bun)* Thank you! I do know, I am bathed and cleansed and dressed. So let us quickly prepare you. But first—let us pray!

(GRANDMOTHER pushes DIXIE and SUSIE down on the floor, lower and lower, with her hands on their heads. She then sinks down on her kneels and begins a loud and powerful prayer.)

GRANDMOTHER: Lord, Lord, Lord. Thank you! —for bringing Susie and Dixie to be with me today. And be with Charles and Doreen as they continue on their journey—now that they have…room! And help Christine not to wear her hair so big. If she wears it so big she might become a harlot! And help Susie and Dixie know not to worry their mother. *(Pushing their heads down further)* If they worry their mother, her arms will SAG! And help them to know that one sheet of toilet paper at a time is sufficient! And Lord, always know the six children were Tyler's idea! And not mine! *(As she begins to stand)* Amen. Amen. Amen. Thank you. Thank you. Thank you!

(As DIXIE runs off)

GRANDMOTHER: Dixie, I do know, you are fast as greased lightning! Now you come and sit in the chair and let Susie plait your hair. What? You don't know how to plait hair? *What? Your mother never taught you how to plait hair?* I do know! How do you wear it when you sleep?

(GRANDMOTHER begins to plait DIXIE's hair.)

SUSIE: Grandmother, no! Grandmother, don't do that to her. You're making her look terrible. She can't go out looking like that!

(As SUSIE is forced into the chair)

SUSIE: Grandmother, NO! My hair's too short!

(When GRANDMOTHER turns away, SUSIE touches her two short braids which stick out on either side of her head. Then, with growing horror:)

SUSIE: Grandmother, what are you doing? Grandmother, no! We go to the First Presbyterian Church every Sunday and Mother never makes us cover our legs. I'm not wearing those old pants Joey left here and neither is she! *(Whispering)* Dixie, say something! Fight! *(To GRANDMOTHER)* Grandmother, I'm NOT wearing those old pants under my dress. Because—those pants are plaid and my dress has flowers in it.

(SUSIE *watches as* GRANDMOTHER *approaches, her eyes grow wide with fright.*)

SUSIE: No, I don't want to see my mother dead and in a casket! No! No! No!! *(She takes the pants and puts them on, sobbing. She then turns and catches sight of both herself and Dixie in a long mirror.)* Dixie! We look — *(As she touches her braids:)* —awful!

(GRANDMOTHER *takes them each by the hand.*)

GRANDMOTHER: Now. Let us enter the House of the Lord! *(Singing)* "When the trumpet of the Lord shall sound and time shall be no more and the morning breaks eternal bright and fair… "

(GRANDMOTHER *is leading them out of her house, through the streets and finally to the Church itself.*)

(End of Scene Four)

Scene Five

(Lights rise on GRANDMOTHER *opening the door of the Church. She is still singing and still clutching* DIXIE *and* SUSIE *by their hands.)*

GRANDMOTHER: *(Singing:)* "When the saved of earth shall gather over on the other shore and the roll is called up yonder, I'll be there!"

(They enter the church and GRANDMOTHER *peers out into the audience, talking to various people.)* Hi there! Do you remember, Doreen, my baby? Well, this are her babies— *(She yanks* DIXIE *and* SUSIE's *hands high above their heads.)* This is Susie and Dixie!

(As the audience responds)

GRANDMOTHER: Thank you! *(To others)* Hi there! These are my granddaughters. *(Lifting their arms again)* This

is Susie! And Dixie! Thank you! *(To another corner)* Hi
there! These are Doreen's girls, Susie and Dixie—

*(*REVEREND THOMPSON *appears and* GRANDMOTHER
smiles at him with pride.)

GRANDMOTHER: Hi there, Reverend Thompson! Do you
remember me?

*(*REVEREND THOMPSON *does.)*

GRANDMOTHER: Well, these are my granddaughters
— *(Almost dislocating their arms above their heads)* Susie
AND DIXIE!! Thank you, Reverend Thompson.

REVEREND THOMPSON: Thank you, Grandmother
Jewel. It is so good to see your young granddaughters
here tonight. *(Under his breath)* What do they have
on? *(To the audience at large)* Looking out I am pleased
to see so many young people in the congregation
tonight because tonight begins the Youth Segment
of our revival! And the message tonight is entitled:
"Daughters of Light—or Daughters of…Darkness!"
(Smiling warmly) You know, I've just been in Claryville
since yesterday. But it seems everywhere I turn I see
signs for a beauty contest Saturday night. A beauty
contest! *(He turns on his heel and goes to his pulpit where
opens an oversized bible. His mood changes to one of rage.)*
Let us turn in our bibles to Second Kings where we
find these words: *(Reading)* "And Jezebel did paint her
face and so they threw her down and her blood was
spattered on the wall and they trod her underfoot.
And when they went to bury her they found no more
of her than the skull and the feet and the palms of
her hands. The dogs did EAT the flesh of Jezebel and
this is the work…of the Lord!" *(He closes the bible and
crosses down to his congregation. He is relaxed and loving.)*
Now, I know what you are thinking. You are thinking
to yourselves: "Why does Reverend Thompson
speak to *us* of Jezebels?" And looking out I see only

good, Godly, young Christian women. I see faces
that plain and unadorned shine with God's beauty.
(Finding SUSIE*)* Little one, what was your name again?
(Listening, then:) Susie! Susie, stand up — and tell all
these people how old you are! *(Under his breath)* What
has she got on? *(Bellowing:)* Twelve years old! Surely
that young face shines with God's beauty! Thank you,
Susie.

(REVEREND THOMPSON *motions* SUSIE *to sit and takes
another look at her get-up.)*

REVEREND THOMPSON: *(To himself)* Pants! She's got
some kind of *pants* on under there. *(Shifting moods)* Is
there anything more precious than a young girl's pure
and Godly face. *(He smiles at* SUSIE *and then points at her
with venomous hate.)* But there is a DEVIL and his name is
SATAN and he HATES your Godly face!! Yes! There is a
Satan and there is a hell and in that hell there is a Lake
of Fire and that fire is ever, ever, ever-lasting! People
try to climb up, up, up out of that Lake of Fire and just
when they get to the top *(He demonstrates.)* Satan comes
and steps on their hands and back down, down, down
they go!
Yes, there is a Satan. And this Satan takes on many
shapes and many guises. He is everywhere at every
time. Let me show you how this Satan works.
Mother—is ironing in the kitchen. *(Demonstrating)*
She has the radio tuned to a gospel station but then
some household chore calls her to another room and
her young daughter happens by— *(He becomes the
daughter.)* —and turns the dial.
SUDDENLY, instead of God's word we have Satan
spitting out lust and before she knows it— *(He begins
a wild, frantic dance.)* —her body begins to gyrate with
Satan's rhythm. But is Satan satisfied with just a dance?
Nooooo. Nooooo!! Now she must dress for him and
paint her face for him and soon she's off to the high

school to be in a beauty contest—*SPONSORED BY THE BOARD OF EDUCATION!* And then she's coming home in the back of some boy's car and then perhaps not coming home at all! And it all began because a radio dial was left *unattended!*

A beauty contest. A beauty contest! What do they do at a beauty contest? *(Striking his chest)* I went! I found out! They parade themselves, almost naked, to all the men of Claryville. *(He parades.)* Look, look, look! *(He struts)* Strut, strut, strut— *(He freezes.)* Touch. Touch. *Touch.* Satan wants your daughters. He's waiting for them in a tube of lipstick.

He's waiting down on Main Street to lure them into the beauty shops!

He wants to pour them into seductive clothing and annoinst their bodies with frankincense and myrrh and Chanel No. 5!

Satan wants your daughters!

And buddy, he gets his prey. Because now these girls are *women!* And these women preen themselves before their God—their mirror! And they gussy themselves with their Jesus—their mascara! And where are they going they preen themselves so?

Straight to hell!

(Sorrowfully) And everyone of these girls in hell is somebody's...daughter. *(Now businesslike)* Now I want to know how many of you sitting here today know some young girl who is going to—roast in hell?

I want to know how many of you sitting here today know that you yourself are in danger of temptation? What? Are you willing to just sit there and let it happen?

Or are you going to stand up—in front of this congregation—stand up—in front of God himself — and say: "No, I will not be a Jezebel!"

Then get off that pew and come down this aisle. Come down this aisle now and say— *(Yelling to the back)* hit it, Sister Miriam! —say "YES" to Gawd! *(Pointing)* I'm talking to you! *(Pointing again)* I'm talking to you! *(Pointing)* I'm talking to YOU!

DIXIE: *(Grinning)* Susie—he's talking to you!

(Convulsed with terror, SUSIE stands and makes her way out of the pew. She goes down the aisle until at last she stands before REVEREND THOMPSON. She is weeping, incoherent.)

SUSIE: No, sir…one time…just one time…my sister's lipstick… sorry…I'm sorry…one time…I didn't mean… *(She glances back over her shoulder, suddenly realizing she is the only person to come forward. She checks over her other shoulder and then, in humiliation:)* Gah!

(SUSIE runs down the aisle and out of the church as the lights fade to black.)

END OF ACT ONE

ACT TWO

Scene One

(A spotlight rises on the adult SUSIE. *She is gazing out into the audience in a reverie.)*

SUSIE: I grew up on a "block". I knew everybody on the block. And if I babysat for them, I knew everything in their medicine cabinet, refrigerator and bookcases. *(Now she is 12 year old* SUSIE*)* There go the Heiney boys. They are the James Dean and Marlon Brando of Claryville! We're not supposed to talk to the Heiney Boys. They're always in trouble. *(Quoting* EULENE*)* "That's what happens when a mother works. *(Pause)* For the phone company. *(Pause)* At *night!"*
The Heiney boys are riding their bikes up and down the street. Without any hands, *(Growing excited:)* without any shirts on. Eating peanut butter and jelly sandwiches. There go the Heiney boys.
Eulene Henderson lives over there. Her middle aged niece lives with her. I wonder what they do over there all day long. They don't have a car, they don't work. They don't go out. I wonder why Roberta lives with Eulene instead of her mother? Eulene does all the work.
I watch her as she hangs out their clothes. She always puts their underwear inside pillow cases. My sisters are practicing the piano. I like to come outside and practice cheers so if anyone rides by they'll know I'm

a sister, too. *(She is suddenly a cheerleader.)* "Beat the Braves! Beat the Braves!" *(She turns her back and shakes her hips.)* "We're going to fight, fight, fight — we're going to fight with all our might!"

(Turning, SUSIE finds the HEINEY boys watching her.)

SUSIE: Duane! What'chall doing around here?

DUANE: *(Almost leering at her)* Bike riding. Hey Wayne, wait up! Wayne, I said wait! Shoo-oot! Wayne's got ants in his pants. *(Leering at her again)* So. Are you going up to the high school tonight to see your sisters in that beauty contest? *(Spitting over his shoulder)* Well. Maybe I'll see you up there.

(DUANE exits. SUSIE stares after him.)

SUSIE: Gah!

(DIXIE leans out of a tree with a pair of binoculars.)

DIXIE: Is it a bird? Is it a plane? No, it's Mrs Susie Duane Heiney!

SUSIE: Dixie, you quit spying on me or I'm telling Mother!

DIXIE: Then I'll tell her I seen you talking to a Heiney Boy! Tsk, tsk, tsk! And I thought you were *SAVED!*

SUSIE: You little brat! You little buck-toothed brat!

(EULENE and MISS MILDRED pass by.)

SUSIE: Hey, Eulene. Hey, Miss Mildred. Ma'am? Yeah, they're getting ready for that beauty contest tonight. They're upstairs now practicing on their talents. Ma'am? Well, I don't know, I just wish they could both win.

EULENE: *(Mournfully)* Wouldn't that be wonderful? *(Suddenly distracted)* Roberta! Put down that hedge clipper! Mildred, she'll kill herself. Roberta, put down those clippers!

SUSIE: Gah. (*Entering the kitchen*) Boy, Mother, everybody and his brother is going to up at the school tonight. (*Shyly, smiling to herself:*) Everybody keeps asking me which one I think's going to win. All the teachers at school—and even Eulene just now.

DOREEN: Uh-huh. Now, who is pulling up in our driveway? (*Squinting*) Oh, it's Bobbi Boland and she's got the girls' dresses! Christine, Dee Dee! Go out and give her a hand. Susie, quick, clear off the table and give her a place to sit down and turn down my beef stew! (*At the door*) Well, come on in, Bobbi! Is that Roger? (*Waving:*) Tell him to come on in, too. Well, I hate to have him just sitting out in the car.

(DOREEN *ushers* BOBBI *and her daughters into the kitchen, closes the door, and begins to hang their evening gowns on the back of the door.*)

DOREEN: Let's just hang the dresses right up here. Ohhh. I can't wait to see the dresses. Is this one Dee Dee's? Dee Dee?

(DOREEN *motions* DEE DEE *over and then removes the plastic covering.*)

DOREEN: Oh, Bobbi! You have outdone yourself! This is beautiful! Run go try it on, Dee Dee. But wait, let's get the shoes. Which ones are the pink ones? (*Opening a box*) Oh, Bobbi, look what a beautiful dye job Roger did. Dixie, run these shoes up to Dee Dee. Now, let's take a look at Christine's. (*She unwraps the second dress.*) Oh, Bobbi! Look at that little bolero jacket! And those tiny stitches. Now, what do you call these shade of green? Just lime? Well, it is beautiful. Christine, run go try it on. Lee-Ann! Take these shoes up for Christine. Now, Bobbi, have a seat. What can I get you? What have I got? How 'bout some iced tea?

BOBBI: Thank yew, Doreen, I'd just *lovvvve* some iced tea! (*Untangling her bracelet*) My charms!

(As DOREEN *gives* BOBBI *a glass of tea)*

BOBBI: Thank YEW, Doreen! *(Snapping her head)* Is there a coaster? Well, I just hate to ruin your pretty table.

(After DOREEN *exits.)*

BOBBI: Hey, Susie, are you going to grow up and be in a beauty contest one day just like your sisters? Susie! Stand up. Come over here. I want you to do something for me. I want you to—walk! —for me. Just from here to here. Stop! It's not your fault. A lot of people don't know it. But there is a secret to walking. You have to—rotate! You have to have—tension. You must always have *TENSION!* You must walk as if you are carrying a penny between your buttocks! Here, let me show you what I mean.

*(*BOBBI *moves* SUSIE *across the kitchen and then begins her walk.)*

BOBBI: Dixie! You know you have a real irritating little laugh? Why don't you go play outside. Susie, aren't you lucky you don't need braces… Now when you decide you are going to learn to… *(Spying* DEE DEE*)* Oh, Dee Dee! You look beautiful! Now, I didn't put the hems in. Your mother can do that. But I'm going to pin them in because I know how they should go. Come on up here in the chair. *(She helps* DEE DEE *up and then begins to pin her the bottom of her dress.)* I like for the hem of the gown to just—kiss—the shoe because that's how I was taught when I was modeling in Atlanta!

(As DOREEN *passes by)*

BOBBI: Hey, Doreen. I was just telling Dee Dee that I like for the hem of the dress to just—grace—the shoe because that's the way I was taught—

(As BOBBI *helps* DEE DEE *down)*

BOBBI: —when I was modeling in Atlanta. *(Spying* CHRISTINE*)* Oh, Christine! Perfect-a-ment-tee-o. No, it's not hemmed. Careful! Just climb up in the chair and I'll pin it in. *(Helping her up:)* I was just telling your mother and Dee Dee that I like for the hem of the gown to just—touch—the shoe because that's the way I was taught when I was modeling—

(Helping Christine down)

BOBBI: —in Atlanta! Now. Do you want to show me your walks again. Okay, Dee Dee, you come first and remember the wire! Oh, Mister Pinocchio!

(BOBBI watches as DEE DEE makes her walk, complete with pivots. BOBBI is not pleased but pretends she is.)

BOBBI: Very good! *(Sighing)* Christine? *(She watches Christine with growing awe and respect.)* Not bad, not bad at all. Okay. All right. First of all, I am not some kind of an oracle. I am not Mohammad coming down from the mountain or anything-like-that. But I have been in a few pageants...thank yew, Christine. It may not seem like much to a lot of other people but I am proud of my titles—thank you. And there are just some rules that apply—and always will apply to pageants. I don't care if it's Miss Claryville High School or Miss Atlanta Peach Blossom—

(Smiling modestly as the girls cheer)

BOBBI: —ya'll cut it out! —or even *Miss America.* Some rules apply and always will. For instance— *IF. FROM THE MOMENT YOU HIT THIS STAGE. YOU DO NOT HONOR THOSE JUDGES WITH YOUR SMILE. AND YOUR POISE. AND YOUR PRESENCE—THEY WILL NOT HONOR YOU WITH POINTS!* Let me let you in on a little secret: *MISS CONGENIALITY NEVER WINS!*

So it doesn't matter what goes on backstage or in the dressing room. It doesn't even matter in the beginning what your talent is, because—*IF—FROM THE MOMENT YOU HIT THIS STAGE—YOU DON'T*

GIVE IT ALL THOSE JUDGES YOU WON'T EVEN BE
IN TOP TEN TO DO A TALENT AND THAT'S JUST
THE WAY THE COOKIE CRUMBLES! (All business)
Dee Dee! You are still having problems with the pivots.
You are making it much more complicated than it
really is. You come to the first pivot and it is one hand.
You come to the second pivot and it is two hands. You
come to the third pivot—*AND THIS IS THE ONLY*
ONE THAT GETS THE LEAST BIT TRICKY—and it is
one hand again!
Do you want me to show you the walk one more time.
(Calming them down) Okay, okay! Is that Roger beeping
for me? *(At the door)* Hey there, Roger-Dodger! Be
right out sweetheart. Okay-y-y-y-y! *(She blows Roger*
a kiss, then gives him a look of murderous rage. She then
glances down at LEE-ANN.*)* Oh, Lee-Ann's not in my
way. You're just fine, hon. *(Almost slinging her away)*
Just come right over here. *(To the girls)* Okay. You
are standing backstage and you hear you name and
number called. You come to the first pivot and it is
one hand— *(Demonstrating)* —and you rock gently
with poise. You come to the second pivot and it is two
hands…now this is risky, but when it works, it *works!*
(Smiling over one shoulder) See? And then you come
to the third pivot it is one hand again and you rock
gently—with poise. See? It is so simple. Both of you
girls come here. I want both to know that I am going
to be sitting out there tonight—yes, *ME,*— sitting in
an audience—just rooting for the two of you! And you
know, if somebody stopped me right out here on Main
Street and said , "well, Bobbi Boland, you're such a fool
about those Van Helms' sisters—which one would you
have win?" I would have to say—I would have to say
that I hope it's a tie — and I mean that! Now get over
here *(Pointing)* because I'm going to give you one last
tip. You too, Susie. And you, Lee-Ann, you're never
too young to learn! *(At the door)* You don't *have to,*

Dixie. *(She turns back to the others and sticks out her front teeth, making fun of Dixie. Then she becomes serious again.)* This is called the Queen Elizabeth. It can be used at any elegant affair, a wedding, a funeral, anyplace where you want to show that extra little bit of class. It is the aristocratic technique of never showing your back when you leave a room. Now some people will just walk right out of a door, like a cow in a barn. *(She demonstrates.)* They don't mean anything by it, they just don't know any better. But you—yes, you, sweetheart! —can add that extra little bit of class if you just find that door with the corner of your eye, and meanwhile you're just taking everybody in—still talking, smiling your brightest bright— *(She is walking backwards, smiling, bobbing her head.)* —and on that, Farewell!!

(BOBBI exits. CHRISTINE rushes to the door to wave her goodbye.)

CHRISTINE: Thank GOD Claryville's got Bobbi Boland. She's the only woman in town with any class.

(CHRISTINE turns, a la BOBBI.)

DOREEN: Christine, get over there and finish peeling those potatoes. As if I have time to hem dresses! *(Glancing out the window)* Now who is pulling up in our driveway? Well, it's probably somebody for you girls and you're just not at home — is that understood? Susie, run outside and see who it is.

TAMMI: *(Mouthing the words)* Why me? *(She goes outside and stares at the car for a long moment and then her eyes widen. She runs back inside and faces the others.)* Mother, it's Grandmother!

CHRISTINE: Grandmother??

DEE DEE: Grandmother????

SUSIE: Yep. It's Grandmother!

(End of Scene One)

Scene Two

(It is two hours later.)

(Lights rise on DALE, *shaving in the bathroom, surrounded by his five daughters.)*

DALE: Christine—if Mama said she'll take care of it, she'll take care of it. *(Distracted)* Dixie! Leave that alone! *(Looking into the mirror)* Well, Dee Dee, that surprises me. We were thinking of sending you to live with her. Ain't that bad, is it, Susie?

(As CHRISTINE *interrupts)*

DALE: Christine…Christine! Mama said she'd take care of it and so we just have to believe she'll take care of it. *(In charge)* Now, get your mind off that and get it where it ought to be. You're gonna be on that stage tonight and I want you to look alive! Get your head up and your shoulders back and don't forget to smile. And don't be worrying about how you look. That's the last thing you've got to worry about— *(Smiling at himself)* —because you've got a good looking daddy! Now clear out of here and let me shave. I've got to look good, don't I, Lee-Ann? Yeah, they may want to crown me!

*(*DALE *is shaving and smiling at his reflection as the lights fade.)*

(End of Scene Two)

Scene Three

(A few minutes later—dinner time)

(Lights rise in the kitchen where the entire family, including GRANDMOTHER, *are seated at the table. They are finishing Grace.)*

DOREEN: …in his name we pray, Amen." *(Replacing her glasses)* Okay. Dee Dee, do you want to start the squash and pass it? Mama, why don't you pass your plate up and let Dale give you some beef stew?

GRANDMOTHER: No, I have plenty of my squirrel meat here. Who wants some of my squirrel meat? *(Offering)* Christine? Well. Dee Dee? I know who wants some of my squirrel meat. *Susie* wants some of my squirrel meat. *(Offering to SUSIE)* I do know WE thank the Lord for this good food. *(Taking a big bite)* And I do know I thank the Lord Brother Ralph for giving me a ride here today. And I trust the Lord will let me stay with you as long as I can to be of service to you!

(DALE leaves the table and goes outside. DOREEN quickly follows him.)

DOREEN: Dale? Dale?? You can't work the way you do and not eat. Dale, another human being cannot make you sick!

(CHRISTINE appears behind them.)

DOREEN: Christine, what is it?

CHRISTINE: *(In tears)* I just want both of you to know tonight is the most important night of my senior year. Dee Dee and I have worked long and hard for this contest—and now she's here and she's going to ruin it. Yes she is, Mother. She is—and you know it!

DOREEN: Christine, I told you I would take care of it. Now, Dale, will you take care of your daughter?!

(DOREEN storms away but pauses outside the kitchen door.) I can't do it all, Lord. I just can't do it all. *(She opens the door, suddenly cheerful.)* Ya'll 'bout through with dinner? Well, you younger girls run go take your baths. *(To GRANDMOTHER)* Now, Mama…

GRANDMOTHER: Here, kit-kit-kit-kit-kitty…

DOREEN: *(Taking the plate)* Mama, we don't have a cat! Mama, Earl Jr. called today. He and Myrna just got through remodeling their family room. Hey! How would you like to go over and see him and Myrna?

GRANDMOTHER: NO! Myrna smokes.

DOREEN: Well…how would you like to go over and visit with Sister Molly Mae?

GRANDMOTHER: Sister Molly Mae's in Georgia. Where are *you* going?

DOREEN: We just have to go up to the school to visit with the girls' teachers.

GRANDMOTHER: Well, I will go with you.

DOREEN: Mama, they just have those hard chairs. Why don't you just stay here? You'd be much more comfortable.

GRANDMOTHER: All right. I will watch over the younger children.

DOREEN: We're all going. No, we don't all have to go, but we all planned to go and we're all going.

GRANDMOTHER: No-o-o-o-o-o-o. Dixie?

DOREEN: Dixie— *(Kneeling down to her)* —would you like to do something for Mama? *(Shocked)* Don't you *ever* pop that retainer out at me again, young lady! Run up those stairs and take your bath!

GRANDMOTHER: I know who will stay with me. *Susie will stay with me!*

CHRISTINE: Please, Susie, please!

DEE DEE: Please! Please!

CHRISTINE: Please?

DOREEN: *(Pitifully)* Sug, would you do it for Mama?

(SUSIE looks from one to the other to the other. Finally:)

SUSIE: Gah.

(End of Scene Three)

Scene Four

(It is one hour later.)

(Lights rise in the kitchen. SUSIE *is washing dishes and* GRANDMOTHER, *perched on a chair next to her, is rinsing.)*

SUSIE: *(Morosely)* Grandmother, you don't have to help me do the dishes. Well, that chair you're leaning on is in my way. *(Glancing right)* Grandmother, we don't save straws...we don't save tinfoil either! *(Watching* GRANDMOTHER*)* If you're going to rinse, don't just use the water in that pitcher. It's all soap. Just turn on the water—

As SUSIE starts to turn on the water, GRANDMOTHER quickly slaps SUSIE's hand away.)

GRANDMOTHER: No!!!!!!!!!!!!! We must save on water. We just take Mister Spoon and Mister Fork and poke them in here *(Poking them into the pitcher)* and they are clean. And now we are done—because we have worked together! *(She drags her chair back to the kitchen table.)* Now, let us do the mending!

SUSIE: *(Bitterly)* Grandmother, we don't have any mending. *(Pause)* Those are just the clothes I brought in from the line. *(Pause)* Those are just my old underwear. *(Pause)* They're supposed to be torn. *(Pause)* I don't know where she keeps the thimble. I don't know where she keeps it! *(But she does. She crosses to the cabinet and yanks open a drawer and plants the thimble on her finger. She crosses back to Grandmother with the thimble in midair.)* Here!

GRANDMOTHER: *(Grabbing the thimble)*

Thank you! Now get a chair and bring it right over
here—next to me! And now look in my sack and find
the Good Book and you can read me a chapter—or
two. Oh, this reminds me of what good fun we used to
have when I was your age. I did the churning. Mama
put me to churning when I was eight. I was a good
churner.

Now sit. And open it. And read—oh read right there.
Right there! *(Murmuring along with* SUSIE*)* Mmmm-
mmmm. He will do it, too. Oh, yes he will! Oh, that is
such a good reading of the Scripture. I wish they could
all be here to hear it. Why did they all have to go to the
high school?

SUSIE: *(Reading)* "It is the wicked whose light is
extinguished…" *(Under her breath)* Because the girls are
in a beauty contest.

GRANDMOTHER: *(Hearing her)* WHO—is in a beauty
contest?

SUSIE: *(Reading)* "The sinner shall suffer saith the Lord."
(Exploding) The girls! Christine and Dee Dee! Both!

GRANDMOTHER: *(Shocked)* That is NOT what your
Mother said.

SUSIE: Well, that's where they are. They're going to
walk across the stage in a bathing suit—almost nekked!

GRANDMOTHER: Sweet Jesus…are they going to show
their legs

SUSIE: To all the men in Claryville, I guess!

(As GRANDMOTHER *gets up)*

SUSIE: What are you doing? Grandmother, you can't go
outside. It's dark out there. It's cold. It's not safe!

GRANDMOTHER: *(Kicking open the door)* The Lord is MY
shepherd!

SUSIE: *(Running after)* Grandmother!!!!!!!!!!!!!!!!!!!!!!!!

(End of Scene Four)

Scene Five

(It is a few moments later.)

(A spotlight rises on EULENE *as she peers through her Venetian blinds.)*

EULENE: Well, Roberta, all's quiet on the Western Front. Come take your turn. Wait! I saw something—running. It's a man. No, it's two men! Get the gun, Roberta, get the gun!

*(*SUSIE *is chasing* GRANDMOTHER *on the street.)*

SUSIE: Grandmother, throw down that antennae! You'll hurt somebody with it!

(Gunshot rings out. SUSIE *screams and throws herself behind a bush.)*

SUSIE: They're shooting at us! Eulene, no! It's not a man. It's me, Susie! Susie!! *(Running to them)* It's my grandmother. She got away! Help me catch her! You go down Seminole and I'll go down Elm. *(Chasing Grandmother again)* Grandmother!!!!!!!!!!!!!!

(We are now center stage at the beauty pageant.)

THE M C: Ho, ho, ho. Thank you, Rhonda Corby, for that amusing anecdote! Her teddy bear! And what a lucky teddy bear! Ha, ha, ha. And now we have— *(Consulting a notecard)* —a serious question! *(Motioning* CHRISTINE *forward)* Miss Christine Van Helms, approach the fishbowl please!

*(*CHRISTINE, *a study in poise and graciousness, crosses to the fishbowl and extracts a folded piece of paper. She opens it and reads the question into the microphone.)*

CHRISTINE: "When does a person become an adult?"

(CHRISTINE *swallows and tries to control the shaking in her hand as she gives the slip of paper to* THE M C. *She peers out into the audience, looking lost until a thought occurs to her which seems to give her sudden confidence.*)

CHRISTINE: (*Quoting:*) When I was as child, I spake as a child, I thought as a child, I understood as a child; but when I became a man, I put away my childish things." (*Gathering steam*) And I think…when you can put away all of your greed…and your hate…and your spite… then…and only then…are you…an…adult! (*As the applause builds*) Thank you! (*Smiling at* THE M C) Thank you! (*Backing up across the stage*) Thank you!!!

(*Back on the streets*)

GRANDMOTHER: I'm coming to save you. I'm coming to save you. I can see the lights! I can see the lights. I'm coming. I'm coming. Oh, Jezebels!

(*Back at the beauty contest*)

THE M C : (*Applauding*) Now, *that* was Claire de Lune! And now we have— (*Consulting his card*) what ho! — more double-trouble from those Van Helms' sisters. We now have Miss Dee Dee Van Helms as soon as she gets her vanity table plugged in— (*Killing time:*) —yes, sir, she's going to be powdering her nose, and then putting on her top hat—and then she's going to ask us— (*Looking over his shoulder*) Ready??— (*She is*) —to give her regards to Old Broadway!!

(*We are back on the streets.*)

GRANDMOTHER: I can see it! I can see it! Get out of my way, Mister Man—

SUSIE: Grandmother, stop hitting the custodian. You'll put out his eye. I'm sorry, Otis. Oh, Otis, help me catch her!

(*At the contest.*)

DEE DEE: *(Singing:)*
"Tell all the gang at 42nd Street
That I will still be there…
(Tap dancing)
Whisper of how I'm yearning,
To mingle with the old time throng
Give My—
(She is executing a buck and wing)
Regards—to—Old—Broadway…"

(Just outside the auditorium, on the steps.)

GRANDMOTHER: I can see the steps, Lord, I can see the steps. *(Shocked)* I do know—children smoking!

(GRANDMOTHER stomps on DUANE's cigarette as SUSIE arrives, out of breath.)

SUSIE: Grandmother! *(Seeing DUANE:)* Duane!

GRANDMOTHER: And now I'm on the steps, Lord. I'm on the steps and I'm going for the door. I will spread your word! I will—

SUSIE: Grandmother, you can't go in there. *(In despair)* Duane, would you please go find my mother?

(SUSIE steps in front of GRANDMOTHER on the steps. With her entire body, she forces GRANDMOTHER back.) You can't go in there! They'll kill me! Are you crazy? You can't go in there…you can't! You can't!

(DOREEN appears at the top of the steps.)

DOREEN: Mama? Susie? *(Glancing back, dismissively)* Thank you, Duane. *(To GRANDMOTHER and SUSIE)* What are you doing here? Come down these stairs and tell me what is going on!

SUSIE: *(Sobbing)* Mother, you always leave me with her. You always do—and it's not fair!

GRANDMOTHER: She said the girls are up here showing their *legs!* You lied!

(DOREEN *looks as if she has been struck.*)

DOREEN: Yes, Mama, I lied. What I should have said—
for a long time now— (*Taking a large breath*) —is this
is our business. (*Pause*) No, Mama, I don't think it's a
sin. What I think is a sin is that you've got me out here
making me miss an important night for my two girls.
Now you can either come in with us, if you can behave,
or you'll just have to go sit and wait in the car.

(DOREEN *and* SUSIE *start off.* DOREEN *take one look and
returns to* GRANDMOTHER *and puts an arm around her.*)

DOREEN: Now, Mama, you know I didn't mean that. I
didn't. Susie? Do you want to go watch?

(SUSIE *zooms up the steps and peers into the window.*)

SUSIE: Mother! Mother!! There's only four girls left and
Christine and Dee Dee are two of them! (*Glancing in
again*) Mother! There's only three girls left—and it's
still Christine and Dee Dee! (*Glancing again*) MOTHER!
It's just Christine and Dee Dee!! They're holding
hands and crying. (*And again*) And now — I can't see.
Everybody's standing up and clapping. (*She begins to
run through the parking lot, electrified.*) Are they coming
out? Are they coming out? Where are they? (*Suddenly
shy*) Hey, Pam. (*She runs across the parking lot, on fire
again as spies* CHRISTINE.) Christine! Christine! Look at
your roses! Did you win?

CHRISTINE: One point. She won by one point. (*Bravely*)
And I'm real happy for her!

SUSIE: Grandmother? Do you want me to help you get
in the car? (*Pause*) Your antennae? (*Searching, then*)
There it is.

(SUSIE *crosses to the antennae, bends down and starts to
pick it up. Someone is helping her. She looks up.*)

SUSIE: Duane!

(SUSIE crosses to GRANDMOTHER and as they start to walk again, SUSIE appears to have a penny in her buttocks. She glances back and smiles at DUANE, a la BOBBI BOLAND.) See ya.

DOREEN: Mama, you get in the back seat with Christine. Dale, is Lee-Ann with you?

(DALE looks into the car at GRANDMOTHER.)

DOREEN: Dale, we'll talk about it when we get home— okay??? *(To a friend)* Well, thank you Mrs Meriweather, your daughter looked lovely, too! Dixie, get down from there. You and Lee-Ann run go crawl in the back-back. Now where is Dee Dee? *(Spying her in the crowd)* Oh my stars—Dee Dee, look at your crown! You look beautiful! *(To a friend)* Well, thank you, Ella. Thank you so much. We'll see you in church! Dee Dee, we need to go now but you can call everybody when we get home, okay?

DOREEN: Why don't you get in the back seat with Mama and Christine?

(DOREEN realizes she has forgotten something. She glances around and sees Susie.) Susie? *(Crossing to her)* You want to slide in between me and Dad? *(As SUSIE slides in)*

SUSIE: *GAH!*

DOREEN: Start the motor, Dad.

(DALE starts the motor and turns on the radio. We hear an instrumental F M song playing softly. He looks into the rearview mirror and sees GRANDMOTHER.)

DALE: *(Muttering)* Yeeooww. *(He glances again and sees his two daughters. Joyfully)* Yeeeooooowwww!!!!

DOREEN: Dale, you're going to hit somebody. Hold on! *(Peering out)* Is that Eulene and Roberta? *(Rolling down her window)* Hey, Eulene! Hey, Roberta! What'chall

doing here? Do what? *(Pause)* Yes— *(Rolling up her window with a vengeance)* —we caught her.
Dale, you are going to hit somebody. Stop. Oh, it's Miss Mildred. She's coming around, she's coming around. *(Rolling down her window)* Thank you, Miss Mildred, thank you so much. Yes, we are. We are proud of them. We sure are! *(She rolls up the window again and glances into the back seat.)* Yes sir, we are proud of Christine and Dee Dee!

GRANDMOTHER: The LORD is proud of me, I do know!

DOREEN: *(Smiling)* Well, Mama, I 'spect he is. *(decisively)* And we're proud of you, too. Yes sir, we are proud of Christine and Dee Dee…and we're proud of Mama. *(Listening)* Yes, Miss Dixie, we're proud of you, too. *(Listening)* Of course we are, Lee-Ann. *(Patting his shoulder)* We're even proud of Dale! *(Her arm around* SUSIE*)* And we're proud of Susie.

*(*SUSIE *looks up at her mother, startled.)*

SUSIE: Huh?

*(*SUSIE *glances sideways at* DOREEN *and the look on her mother's face fills her with joy.)*

SUSIE: Gah!

*(*SUSIE *is now looking up through the windshield, marveling at the night sky. She is riding on air as the lights fade to black.)*

(Curtain)

END OF PLAY

www.ingramcontent.com/pod-product-compliance
Lightning Source LLC
Chambersburg PA
CBHW070033110426
42741CB00035B/2753